I last winter saw...
on a spre...
And it put me...
and imag...

— WALT WHITMAN

D1733143

CROSSING BORDERS

Poems by
STEVE KOWIT

Drawings & Watercolors by
LENNY SILVERBERG

© 2010 by Steve Kowit and Lenny Silverberg
All rights reserved.

ISBN: 978-1-933132-74-7
First Edition

Spuyten Duyvil
800-886-5304
http://www.spuytenduyvil.net

For inquiries about Lenny Silverberg's art,
contact: nonilenny@gmail.com

To Jackie Ledler —
with friendship
Steve Kowit June 1, 2010

DEDICATION

Lenny Silverberg dedicates
this book to his wonderful
daughter Kim and his loving,
very, very sweet wife, Noni.

Steve Kowit dedicates this
book to his beloved wife
Mary; to the spirit of Rachel
Corrie; to the courageous
Palestinian, Jewish, and
international volunteers of
the International Solidarity
Movement; and to refugees
everywhere.

CONTENTS

INTRODUCTION

by ROBBIE CONAL

Lenny and Kowit.
Together again...
Far Out!
I've known these two grizzled wizards a long time.
Longer than they've known me...

September 1961:

I show up to register for classes at Brooklyn College, almost 17 years old, an embryonic hipster fresh out of the High School of Music & Art, but wrung out from working in the Catskills all summer where I was schooled in the art of waiting on animals by none other than post-beat poet/playwright, Murray Mednick whose paraphrased wisdom was: "eat everything, fuck everything, forget everything." Unbeknownst to me—that summer in bucolic Hell—Mednick was one of the growling young lions in the writing program at Brooklyn College.

My first day at B.C. I hit a red brick wall. All the art classes seem like they're third grade "Teachers' Ed." No can do. What's up with B.C.'s reputation as a heavy art school? Isn't the legendary absolutist, Ad Reinhardt, supposed to be teaching something about nothing here? And Jimmy Ernst, the hepcat son of Max—did he get raptured, leaving just his wig hat on the too perfect, fresh mown lawn? Maybe "reputation" means the past. Whatever, this course of retro-action could severely jeopardize the shape of my not-quite-jelled cool.

By lunchtime I'm following a smoldering, dark,

older (everyone was older), beatnik witch—black turtle-neck, black tights, hoop earrings, Fred Braun leather shoes and handbag, kohl eye shadow, the works—around campus. I'm sure she thought she was being stalked by a puppy dog with a gun in his pocket.

Wisely, she leads me off campus to the local dive, *The Sugar Bowl* luncheonette, the Cedar Bar of B.C.'s Flatbush hood. Home away from home of the blazing literary lights and art stars on campus. Seniors. Legends:

The acerbic wise guy poet who hung with Stanley Kunitz in the Village, Steve Kowit.

The redhead who crossed ironic, poison-tipped paint brushes with Ad Reinhardt, Lenny Silverberg.

My benevolent witch had simply laid me off on her boys; their booth was her personal lost and found department.

The Legends looked me up and down... Nothing.

I was gone. Deep into my own Ralph Kramden, "Hummina-hummina-hummina" moment. Just as I was about to skulk away, one or the other of them bailed me out, "Hey little buddy, order the chicken salad on a Kaiser...and get your tiny arty ass over here." Something like that.

The rest of the semester they put me on a short leash and dragged me through the East Village scene. Art. Music. Poetry. Cheap dope. All that, I'm sure. But all I remember is JAZZ: Monk, Coltrane, Ornette, Cecil Taylor, Albert Ayler.

I was underage and squeaky, so once they'd hustled me into a club, Lenny would whisper, "Shut the fuck up. Sit on your hands... and *listen*." It was the quietest I've ever been. It was the greatest music I've ever heard.

Of course my hipster mentors also managed to leave me high and dry in several dicey situations. Like at 1 am, sitting on a hardwood floor at a candlelit, fifth floor-walk-up-rent-party in Alphabet City, featuring beatniks, bongos and junkies. It was past my bedtime. I looked around. There was so much smoke, I couldn't see a thing. Didn't matter— my guys were long gone like a turkey through the corn.

Shit like that. All part of my education. Besides, their night was just beginning.

A hundred years later, here we are.

Kowit: Still the most raging, socially concerned, funniest dead serious poet I've ever met.

Silverberg: Still the most soulful, funniest, most intractable painter of what he calls "interchangeable suffering" I know.
(Lenny, this is a compliment.)

They want me to write something about something. Maybe because I'm the only person they know who still owes them. Maybe not.

We get some stories going. After Lenny recounts one of his classic Monk Five Spot episodes, Kowit, mulling it over, turns to him and says, "Did I know Robbie then? I don't remember him being there."

I get that a lot.

After high school, they were responsible for almost

every meaningful cultural experience I had in New York—before they told me to leave (as in, drop out of Brooklyn College) "for your own good." Like, I was in the midst of telling Lenny the kind of paintings I wanted to make, when he doubled-up in pain—*from laughing so hard*—and, barely squeezing the words out (spitting all over me), said, "This is not the place for you." Point taken.

Still, we perpetrated a lot of culture—or at least they did and I watched—in the short time I stood in for *Zelig* in that crowd. However, just about every cool scene I remember, one of them says I wasn't there.

So when Lenny and Steve showed up with this tough, poignant collaboration: drawings and poems addressing the international epidemic of refugees—chronic, involuntary global *nomadism* caused by tribal, racial, religious and predatory economic one-upmanship (also known as *disaster capitalism*)—and asked me if I was *with them* on this one... I thought they were putting me on, as usual.

Although Steve and Lenny still carry their sharp-edged, New York wise-guy DNA like cement chips on their shoulders, they immediately shot back a stereophonic, "No jokes, this isn't funny!"

Indeed.

So, when you skip this intro and get into the art, you won't find any yuks along the lines of, "A Priest, a Rabbi, a Monk, a Muslim Imam and an involuntary nomad walk across the desert, into a bar...."

No funny here.

Although humor can be a switchblade of critical deconstruction and these guys can swing it with the best of them, right here, right now, they're going for soul. Cutting deeper.

So get ready. They render a double dose, slicing to the bone with achingly fine-tuned artistry. Kowit and Silverberg have each honed their characteristic styles down to a focused, reductive form—accomplished *contrarianly* (as is their wont) by addition.

Kowit plus Silverberg equals way more than two. Yet together, they reduce abstract social, political and economic issues to something more basic: representational humanity.

R.B. Kitaj once wrote, "Art needs a job."

No shit.

Here it is: Making better metaphors.

Lenny has made a great one: He draws lines of baggage. Literally and figuratively. Recently, by way of explanation— or something—he told me, "I draw baggage from my head."

This can be taken in several ways. Lenny has a unique way of expressing himself, whether he's using words or images. Even though it might sound funny, I prefer to think of his explanation as a trick bag of possibilities. While addressing his personal issues, it certainly contains more than his own psychological baggage. So do these drawings.

The *history* of human baggage is in Lenny's art. Which is where his concept of *interchangeable suffering* is coming from. Question: How do lines of human baggage become an interchangeable metaphor?

Answer: Art history.

The idea is that a drawing of a line of, let's say, Iraqi refugees and their baggage—if composed with a delicate balance of historically informed elements, both technically formal and emotionally expressive — can also stand in for lines of refugees trekking out of Kosovo, Darfur, Afghanistan, Eastern Europe, wherever, whenever — throughout human history. To my eyes, even echoing the Israelites' exodus from Egypt.

Lenny knows art history. (He has almost as many artists' monographs in his loft as he has jazz LP's.) He's parsed it for emotive content and use value. His artistic influences range from the obscure—Il Guercino, a late Italian Renaissance painter—to Tiepolo, Goya, Rembrandt and back to the underappreciated Ludwig Meidner (German, 1884-1966), especially his self-portraits. In his studio one night last winter, riffling through a book of Meidner's drawings, Lenny paused at a particularly unraveled visage. The title of the drawing, *"I, Battered Lump of Clay"* (1917—think about it). The use of representational distortion for expressive effect is the basis of German Expressionism. What it expresses is pain. Art history *is* cultural baggage.

No poet establishes a scene more vividly than Steve Kowit. It's his voice—transcribing hauntings. A crunch of sneakers on gravel. A rattle of bones. A mind-bending marathon bus ride: Neal Cassady noir. A Southeast Asian jungle fever nightmare lost in Brooklyn. "History riffling its pages." And breaking your heart.

I "read" this picture book months ago, but I can still hear *the voice* with echoes of Ginsberg and Kunitz, but utterly personal to the point of confessional; also matter-of-factly—specifically—accusatory, yet empathetic. Global. Wherever you live, it'll come get you and—personally—take you along on its Dantesque roller coaster ride, rumbling on down through past and present world history.

Just looking at the cover of this art-poetry book, I felt like I was in line at a global soup kitchen, waiting my turn—not to eat, but to jump into the pot. Once dunked, the roiling, boiling soup's undertow dragged me around the planet, swimming with illegal immigrant workers and in-over-their-heads basic training newbies, treading water under bridges overburdened with innocents fleeing the bombs of the beaten (ironically) most powerful army in the world. Gasping, I found myself beached over and over again—homeless on every landmass we call home. Including Steve's backyard. What a trip!

Oh, by the way, one Kowit caveat: The past isn't the past. Not with Steve. With him? It's inside him. Maybe that's his point: No escape. No little house tucked away on the prairie; no white picket fence is going to keep us high and dry. Not now.

More than ever before, we're all in the soup together, no matter how we got here or what part of the bowl we occupy. If you're not an involuntary immigrant, one will find you and you'll have to deal. Take a war —there are so many to choose from—take mine...please. War will find you and, if it doesn't drive you out of your home, it will drive you out of your mind.

By the third pair of poems and drawings, all of us have been issued camo fatigues, we're feeling the effects of lugging a deconstructed yurt around the world or at least we've learned how to balance our luggage on our heads.

If this seems a tad vague or flip to you, here's an angle of penetration that's haunted me since I got into this powerful little book:

When addressing chronic global issues—instead of obsessively adjusting algorithms that juggle ideology, politics, class, race, cost/benefit ratios and profit margins— we might have a real chance to solve them if we would just include all of humanity in the solution. As for refugees from whatever, wherever: *they are us*. Inevitably bringing to mind the Yiddish word, *krekhts*—best articulated by the expression, essentially a sigh, "Oy..." (As in, "Oy gevalt!"). It's a deep moan that is, as Michael Wex eloquently put it, "...the involuntary physical reaction to the revelation of...the difference between things as they are and as they're sup- posed to be."

Krekhts also happens to be the Yiddish term used to denote the "sob" that's a characteristic of klezmer music. In this, at least, Yiddish—standing in for the Jewish Diaspora—is not alone.

That sad, soulful reactive moan has global commonality. In other words in other cultures it's called the blues, *duende* (Spain), *zaghareet* (Middle East), *ílílta* (East Africa), *irrintzi* (Basque) and *ulu-uli* (Bengali). All places where refugees have either gone to or come from or both.

ROMERO

By early December the dirt road will be nicely macadamed,
& the backcountry dust will no longer blow through the window
into my hair. In the chill of the oncoming winter
I'll rise from my chair & throw pitch-pine & oak on the fire—look,
it is nearly winter already! By now Romero
should either be up around Fresno, working construction,
or back in Tuxtla Gutierrez, yoked to a cart of *paletas*,
& mending his socks—& plotting another go at the States.
When he stepped from the canyon I pulled to the shoulder
& opened the door. We were north of Tecate: the border patrol
swarming over the highway. Did I have any neighbor,
he wanted to know, who needed a worker?
So all morning, at my place, we cut back the wild chamise
by the shed, though we ended up arguing over money:
   he wouldn't take a cent—that was to pay
    me for picking him up
     in the first place. "Romero, for god sakes
     you can't work for nothing!"—
    & kept at him until he relented.
    Mary, what fine enchiladas! what heavenly pears!
    How exhausted he was, & dusty
     & hungry & hopeful!

Late in the evening we wove our way out of the mountains:
the Barrett grade thru Dulzura down to Spring Valley & north to Santee.
It was August. The night sky a bucket of coins spilling over the hills.
Now & then meteors flared thru the darkness & vanished.
"Right here is good," he said on a back street, at a grove of black
eucalyptus. I pulled to the curb. It was where he would sleep.
In the morning, a truck cruising Magnolia would take him to Fresno,
where *la migra* was scarce & plenty of guys like himself,
without papers, were working construction. He slung his blanket
over his shoulder, picked up his bag, & asked me again
in his broken, measured, tentative English, please to thank
my *María bonita* for all of her kindness. I said that I would.
"Romero, take care...." & under those fugitive stars
we gave each other a long, final *abrazo*. Country
of endless abundance & workers with nowhere to sleep.
"Esteban, I...." — & he nodded, & turned,
& walked off into that tunnel
of trees & was gone.

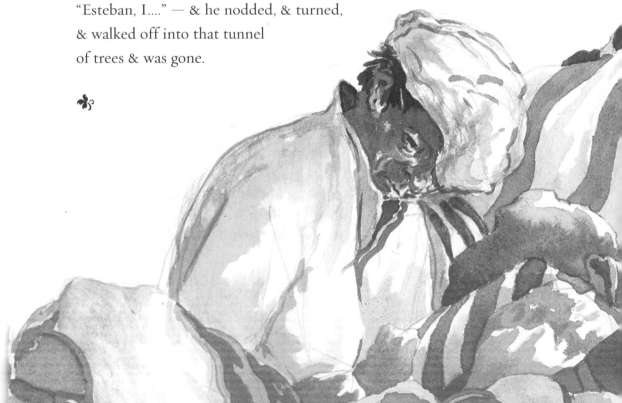

BASIC

The first thing that they do is shave your head
    & scream into your face until you drop
        the pleasant fiction that had been your life.
      More quickly than you would have guessed
     you learn obedience: to shut your mouth
        & do what you are told; that you survive
          by virtue of compliance, shutting down.
           When they scream, "drop for twenty,"
        then you drop.
          If wobbly from lack of sleep,
            you're told to sit up half the night & strip
              your M-1 down, that's what you do.
              You strip it down.
              The only insubordination's
            in your eyes, that can't
             accept the order not to close.
         Your combat boots
          kept so compulsively spit-shined
        you see your face in both hard toes–skinned
      to the scalp, pathetically distorted,
       not unrecognizable but not quite you–
        a self that marches dutifully through
       sleet & has perfected the low crawl.
         One gray morning in the second week
     of basic training, lacing up his boots,
      that shy, phlegmatic, red-haired boy who bunked
     above me whispered,

"Steve,

I don't believe I'm gonna make it...."

"No way, man! You're doing fine! Hey look,

c'mon, we're late,"

& shrugged him off to race out just in time

to make formation in the mist

of that Kentucky morning.

He was right. He didn't. He took

a razor blade that night,

& crawling underneath the barracks

slashed his throat.

What little of myself I saved in there

I saved by tiny gestures of defiance:

Instead of screaming *Kill*, I'd plunge

my bayonet into that dummy screaming

Quill... Nil....

At rifle drill I'd hum the *Internationale*

& fire fifty feet above the target. I kept Dexedrines

in my fatigues. Took heart from the seditious drollery

of Sergeant May, that L.A. homeboy

with the black goatee, all hip panache & grace:

that bop salute and smart-ass version of left face.

& sometimes from his cadre room at night, the wailing

blues of Ray Charles drifted through the barracks,

& I'd lie there in the dark, awake—remembering

that other life that I had left behind.

& it was Sergeant May & Ray Charles

& Dexedrine that got me through.

Had I been more courageous, less the terrified recruit
who did what he was told, I would have hung back
with that boy & argued with him,
said whatever needed saying
or at least have heard him out, just listened, or let
someone know... or somehow, god knows, saved him.
But I wasn't. & I didn't.
I was just a kid myself.
For all my revolutionary rhetoric, I shut my eyes
& ears, when shutting of the eyes & ears was politic.
When they said strip your M-1 down, I stripped it down.
When they said march, I marched.

TAEDONG RIVER BRIDGE

In memory of Jerry Greenberg

Retreating, Walker's 8th Army torched whatever
lay in its path, battered Pyongyang
with mortars & rockets till the whole
besieged city crumbled in flame.
Blew up the granaries, too, & the bridges & roads,
so that those who didn't freeze to death
would be sure to die of starvation—vengeance
against the Chinese Red Army & the peasant
armies of North Korea for beating them back
to Inchon. The U.S. command shelling that city
till nothing remained but that one standing bridge:
tangle of girders with hardly a place to find footing
& nothing to hold as it swayed in the sleet
of the wind over those waters—Taedong
River Bridge, the only way left, short of death,
to cross out of Pyongyang. Ten thousand
terrified souls swarming over its splintered ribs.
On their backs, in their arms, whatever they owned
or could carry. Women cradled their infants.
Men strapped what they could to their shoulders.
The crippled & dying & blind inching their way,
for to slip—& hundreds of those fleeing slipped—
was to vanish into the icy hell of that river.
Then the others would clutch one another & wail
in that other language of theirs, while
they kept moving. What else could they do?

For what it was worth, those who fell through
saved the lives of those inching behind them,
letting them know where not to step next.
                                        Jerry,
    that's what you did for me, too.
        Now & again, that awful black limo pulls up
                            at the curb in front of our house back in Flatbush,
                    & Henrietta, your mother, steps out, gaunt
                        as death in that black cotton shawl
                            while I watch from an upstairs window.

Then my own beloved mother slips into the room,
lays a hand on my shoulder, & tells me, quietly,
lest I say the wrong thing when her dearest friend
enter the house, what she had hoped never
to have to tell me at all:

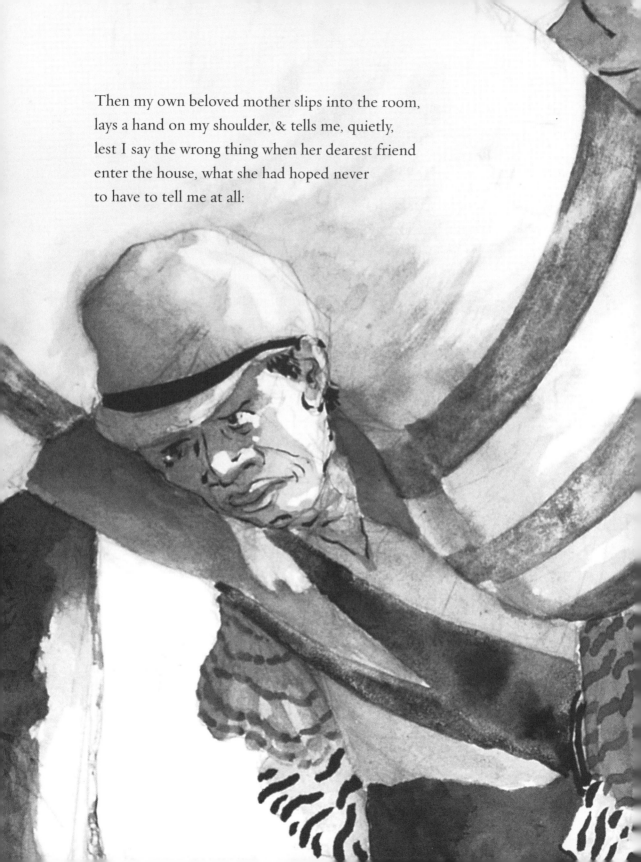

that you had been killed at the front.
I was twelve. Forty years later I remain stunned.
Now & again, something triggers it back
& I drift out to Kelly Park
& watch you fastbreak downcourt—
that long, floating jump from the corner.
The swish of the net.

                    Jerry, I don't know you'd care,
but when my number came up for the next
             imperial bloodbath I gave my draft board
                the finger—for us both. & for every last

                  terrified soul on both sides.
                  I can't tell you how grieved I am still that you're gone.
                  Or thank you enough for the warning: your death
                  letting me know where I stand, who my real
                  enemies are, what the heavy money
                  had in store for me too.
                  In a way, then, I owe you my life: more than anyone
                  else, you were the one who showed me
                  where not to step next—the one up ahead,
                  in the bitter wind of the past, who fell through.

              ❧

BUKOVINA

When they wearied of tromping from house to house gunning
them down one by one, the German & Romanian troops
rounded up all the Jews who were left in the village, marched
them to the banks of the Bug River, & shot those too.
According to the novelist Aharon Appelfeld, who had returned
to the ravishing landscape of his boyhood so that he might
stand at last where his beloved mother & grandmother
lay buried, a peasant woman who had witnessed everything
swore that the dirt-covered pits had trembled for several days.
"For years I had tried to draw my mother out of the harsh darkness
where she lay," Appelfeld writes in the excerpt from his memoir
that appeared in the *New Yorker* the week I returned from
the deathbed of my own beloved mother, sitting
beside her as she lay delirious &
dying in a hospital back east.
In that same issue there were
two amusing cartoons
& an austere poem by Louise Glück
concerning Dido's fatal passion
for Aeneas back in ancient
Carthage, which Rome,
unquenchable
in its vengeful fury,
had laid siege to &
destroyed. Armenia,
I thought to myself,

& Nagasaki. No Gun Ri. The Congo
& Tasmania. Rwanda, I thought. & Sabra, Ramla, Deir Yassin…
I set the article aside, shook myself free of it, & went about
my business, getting done some part of what I had intended
to get done. But two days later picked it up again
& brought it back into my study. & there, the door shut,
the rug still littered with photos of my family, photos taken
back when everyone was young, fading snapshots
of my folks, just kids on ice skates on their honeymoon,
& dancing arm in arm up in the Catskills decades later
— photos that I hadn't yet had time to sort — I read the piece
again until I came to it, that sentence I'd been looking for.
Outside, it was already dark. Appelfeld had been a boy
of eight when the German & Romanian troops
had entered the village of Drajinetz & "with the cooperation
of the local population," had wiped out the Jews. I sat there,
staring at those photos at my feet & then, despite myself,
went back & read that sentence yet again: the one
about those pits into which the dead & dying had been flung,
those pits that had trembled, the woman swore, for several days.

❧

CHECK THE MAP

Let's all take a deep breath and repeat after me: Give war a chance.
This is Afghanistan we're talking about. Check the map. It's far away.

—Thomas Friedman, *NY Times*

But what if tomorrow, turning the corner, it's not that
familiar street with those elegant two-story homes
& luxurious lawns, but a gutted-out havoc of empty
doorframes, & the ruins of what must have been walls.
Overhead, the shrieks of B52s diving back thru the clouds.
A smothering haze thru which you see women in burkhas
down on their knees digging their dead from under
the rubble. Two blocks from home & it's suddenly
Kandahar, the Kapisa Valley, Mazar-i-Sharif.
That wreaking of vengeance you were so pleased
to watch on TV. But it's you now who cannot stop
coughing, whose mouth has dropped open in terror,
whose eyes smart in that acrid smoke; you
who are scurrying, shuddering, hugging the shadows.
Till you manage, somehow, at last, to find your way home:
that snug little duplex with its little flag decal hung
on the window over the door. Still shaking, you get the key
in the lock & stumble into your favorite chair. But it's hours
before your heart stops pounding inside your chest
& you're able to breathe, till you no longer retch over
the toilet, till you've got yourself stable & calm, & all but
convinced it must have been some sort of vertigo, seizure,
delirious dream. But now, thank the Good Lord, you've
come to your senses at last, & are more or less clear who
you are, where you live, what it is you're supposed to believe.

❦

TRANS-AMERICAN EXPRESS

Regaling us with stories
 of her epic bus excursion
  from the west coast to Manhattan,
   Pat, the O.B. go-go dancer,
    mentioned that a pal of hers from Reno
     earned a living one lean season
      giving head
       on the back seat
        of the cross-country Greyhound,
         which got me thinking

of all those second-class Mexican buses,
the ones that were decked out like altars
with fringe-festooned windows
& plastic flowers
& votive candles
& the Virgin of Guadalupe
over the brilliantined head of the driver,
& how we would hurtle over
      precipitous backwater roads
        to end in those sleepy towns
         full of jacarandas & dust:
           a burro in shade by a wall,
           the vultures wheeling above us,
            invisible Indian women with infants
            begging in doorways,
          kids with yellow boxes of Chiclets
           walking the streets all afternoon
            for twenty centavos.
             That Pichucalco run, remember?
             Quetzaltenango, where we froze all night.
             Dusk on that white washboard road
             in Quintana Roo: hunters
             drifting like wraiths thru the mist.
             Laconic *chicleros*
              insisting we take their seats to stay dry
              in the teeming Peten
               on that bus with the busted windows.
               Tikal — the ruins of white temples

in the jungle, monkeys
howling in the trees,
incredible starlight & rain
& then to get stranded
　crossing the Rio Dulce back —
　　sixteen hours of stolid mestizos
　　　with bracelets of chickens.
　　　　& south over the Andes — the bus
　　　　to Tumaco, Riobamba, Pomasqui,

Huancayo to Cuzco...
& once, in that Andean vast,
before dawn, in Peru,
on the *altiplano*, in moonlight,
plowing our way thru the dust,
a herd of vicuña, most delicate
of God's creatures, turning as one
in that ancient silence
to watch us... or bless us....
Pat's L.A. to New York bus saga
bringing it back to me here
in this other life in the States
where the Greyhounds
humming over the freeways
   are disinfected with Lysol at night
       till they're perfectly spotless,
         & sport their own little toilets
          & interchangeable drivers
          & the American dream is made manifest:
       to be blown in the back seat
        by a showgirl from Reno
          while racing into the winking,
           libidinous eye of that fabulous city—
          the one we've been heading out
        for all of our lives,
        that spasm of throbbing lights
        in the unapproachable distance,
        luring us on.

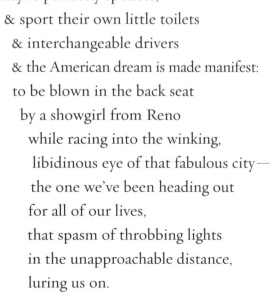

REFUGEES, LATE SUMMER NIGHT

Woke with a start, the dogs
barking out by the fence,
yard flooded with
light. Groped my way
to the window.
Out on the road a dozen quick
figures hugging the shadows:
bundles slung at their shoulders
& water jugs at their hips. You
could hear, under the rattle of
wind, as they passed, the crunch of
sneakers on gravel. *Pollos.* Illegals
who'd managed to slip past the
Border Patrol, its Broncos
& choppers endlessly circling the
canyons & hills between here & Tecate.
Out there, in the dark, they could have
been anyone: refugees from Rwanda,
slaves pushing north.
Palestinians, Gypsies, Armenians, Jews....
The lights of Tijuana, that yellow
haze to the west, could have
been Melos, Cracow, Quang Ngai....
I watched from the window till they were lost in
the shadows. Our motion light turned itself off.
The dogs gave a last, perfunctory bark
& loped back to the house: those dry, rocky hills

& the wild sage at the edge of the canyon
vanishing too. Then stared out at nothing.
No sound anymore but my own breath,
& the papery click of the wind in the leaves
                    of that parched eucalyptus: a rattle
                    of bones. Chimes in a doorway.
                    History riffling its pages.

WILL BOLAND & I

stroll from Dog Beach down to Cape May, grumbling
over this nation's inexhaustible
predilection for carnage: the mask of rectitude
painted over the skull of vindictive rage.
It is midwinter, the beach all but deserted:
an elderly gent walks an elderly golden retriever;
a family of four is out hunting for shells;
two good old boys chugging their Michelobs
take in the last of the sunset:
down at their feet, Iwo Jimaed into the sand,
a colossal American flag
that they've lugged down here to the beach
with their cooler of beer to cheer on the home team.
Night & day, on the other side of the world,
daisy-cutters are pounding a village
to shambles, bathing the landscape in blood.
Women crouch in the rubble rocking their dead.
Listen, I say to Will.
E. O. Wilson can swear up & down there are species
of ants even more compulsively genocidal
than man: I, for one, remain unconvinced.

Above us, that gorgeous midwinter dusk:
At our feet, the Pacific, ablaze in magentas & red.
True, Steve, he ventures. *But still you've got*
to admit we're just as much a part of this world
as anything else...& maybe,

in some crazy way, marvelous too!
    I shrug.
We walk on in silence.
A couple of high-school girls,
frolicking in & out of the surf, smile up at us sweetly.
A part of this world, yes, I snarl back.
But surely the ugliest part! the words hardly
out of my mouth when those two young women,
now twenty yards or so down the beach,
suddenly fling open their arms, rise to their toes,
leap into the air, & float there — angelic... unearthly...
impossibly luminous creatures, alighting
at last in a dazzle of pirouettes & glissades,
only to rise up into the air again & again, while Will
& I stand there — dumbfounded, grinning, amazed.
Under the flare of the night's first stars
each *grande jeté* more splendid, rapturous,
vaulting! Two ardently schooled young ballerinas,
silhouetted against the indigo flames
of the darkening western horizon.
The last of the light of this world
setting behind them.

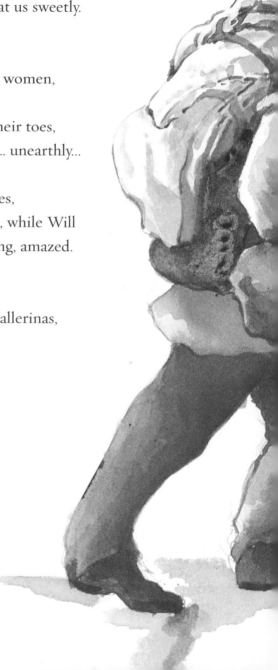

BIOGRAPHIES

Lenny Silverberg and Steve Kowit met in 1960 when they were students at Brooklyn College where Lenny was studying in the Art Department with the painters Ad Reinhardt, Burgoyne Diller and Robert Henry, and Steve was studying linguistic philosophy with John Hospers and Martin Lean. They both contributed to the Brooklyn College Art and Literature Magazine, *Landscapes*, of which Lenny was art editor in 1961-62.

In 1962, after Steve's Conscientious Objector petition was denied by the Coney Island Draft Board, the two friends entered the U.S. Army Reserves and did their basic training together at Fort Knox, Kentucky. After their release from active duty, both lived for several years on New York's Lower East Side and remained close friends. During the next 3 years Lenny decided he wasn't an Abstract painter, which his training had prepared him to be, and he taught himself to paint and draw figuratively. Steve studied poetry with Stanley Kunitz and Robert Lowell but, more importantly, was honing his craft at the lively coffee house poetry-reading venues of the Lower East Side.

In 1965, Lenny went to study at the University of Mexico and to learn from the murals of Rivera, Orozco and Siqueiros. Steve moved to San Francisco to try to get the army off his back, to escape the endless police sirens of Lower Manhattan, to do graduate work, and to see if it was really true that San Francisco was Paradise. Shortly afterwards, Lenny joined him in the Bay Area where they shared a flat in the Haight-Ashbury and later had apartments a few doors away from each other in the Fillmore district. During those years Lenny became involved in the psychedelic art and music scene. He contributed art to Allen Cohen's *San Francisco Oracle* (sweet Allen Cohen, recently deceased, was a friend of them both from Brooklyn College days), and was a member of the light show ensemble that included artists and filmmakers such as Bruce Conner, Robert Comings, Howard Fox, Roger Hillyard and Ben Van Meter. Their light shows became an integral part of the dances at the Avalon Ballroom and were featured at multimedia events at The San Francisco Museum of Modern Art and other venues.

Both Lenny and Steve left San Francisco around 1968, but Lenny subsequently returned and taught at the DeYoung Museum Art School, the California College of Arts and Crafts, and in the Department of Architecture at the University of California. He participated in several group shows and had one-man shows at the DeYoung Museum in San Francisco, The College of Notre Dame in Belmont, the University of Connecticut, and more recently at the Overtones Gallery in Los Angeles. He is represented in the permanent collections of the San Francisco Museum of Art, The California Palace of the Legion of Honor in The Achenbach Foundation, the Grundwald collection at UCLA and the Library of Congress. Lenny and his wife Noni returned to New York in 1984 and they now divide their time between Manhattan and their home in Los Ojos, New Mexico.

Steve left San Francisco on the advice of his lawyer, after he had sent a letter to the army informing the government that if he fought in Vietnam it would be for the other side. Steve and his beloved wife Mary lived off and on for the next several years in Mexico, Central and South America. They eventually returned to the States where he taught at various colleges, worked as an editor for a Florida publisher, and eventually settled in San Diego where he taught at a number of colleges and universities and founded that area's first animal rights organization. He is the recipient of a National Endowment Fellowship in Poetry, two Pushcart Prizes, and several other awards. His books include *In the Palm of Your Hand: The Poet's Portable Workshop*; a translation of Neruda's *Incitement to Nixonicide and Praise for the Chilean Revolution*; and several collections of his own poetry including, most recently, *The Gods of Rapture* published in 2006 (cityworkspress.org), and *The First Noble Truth* published in 2007 by the University of Tampa Press.

In this, their third collaboration, Lenny Silverberg and Steve Kowit are joined by motion/graphic designer Deborah Ross, and by her husband, the well-known political artist Robbie Conal, whose essay introduces this book.

ACKNOWLEDGMENTS

"Romero," "Basic," and "Refugees" were published in Steve Kowit's collection *The Dumbbell Nebula,* Heyday Press (2000); "Trans-American Express" was published in his collection *Lurid Confessions,* Carpenter Press (1986); "Will Boland & I" was published in his collection *The First Noble Truth,* U Tampa Press (2006). "Taedong River Bridge" was published in an interview with Steve Kowit in *Triplopia* (online) and in *The Sun,* which magazine also published "Will Boland & I." The poems "Bukovina" and "Check the Map" are published here for the first time.

All drawings and watercolors are owned by the artist, Lenny Silverberg. Except for a few which have been included in group shows, they have not previously been shown.